FREEHAND SKETCHING

In the architectural environment

Kingsley K. Wu

VNR VAN NOSTRAND REINHOLD
_____ New York

Printed in the United States of America

Designed by Kingsley K. Wu

Van Nostrand Reinhold
115 Fifth Avenue
New York, New York 10003

Van Nostrand Reinhold International Company
Limited
11 New Fetter Lane
London EC4P 4EE, England

Van Nostrand Reinhold
480 La Trobe Street
Melbourne, Victoria 3000, Australia

Nelson Canada
1120 Birchmount Road
Scarborough, Ontario M1K 5G4, Canada

14 13 12 11 10 9 8 7 6 5 4 3 2 1

Library of Congress Cataloging-in-Publication Data

Wu, Kinsgley K., 1934-
  Freehand sketching in the architectural environ-
ment/Kingsley K. Wu.
      p.   cm.
  ISBN 0-442-00296-3
      1. Drawing—Technique. 2. Architecture—
Sketch-books. 3. Buildings in art. I. Title.
NC825.B8W8   1990
720'.28'4—dc20   90-30340
                                          CIP

To my mother, AMY H. WU,

late of Butte, Philadelphia, Shanghai,
Bangkok, and Tokyo:

Don't worry, Mom, it's okay for me to be
drawing pictures all the time.

My thanks to Editor Everett Smethurst, Alberta Gordon, Managing Editor, and all the good people at VNR for allowing me to do this book my way.

Much appreciation to my colleagues Terry Postero for her support and advice during an early review, and to Lind Babcock for help on the technical end of publishing.

Special thanks to Margery Lang, Editor par Excellence, for all the Harvard commas, defining and nondefining relative pronouns, and encouraging remarks.

Above all, thanks to my wife, Susan, for putting up with me in all the years of trudging through cities and towns, up hills and down, in and around buildings and even flying buttresses, so that I could experience the architectural environment.

Some of the sketches from northern Spain were done under a grant from the United States-Spain Joint Committee for Cultural and Educational Cooperation.

CONTENTS:

INTRODUCTION

For people who are involved with designing the physical environment — particularly those who are in architecture, interior and product design, landscape or city planning — the ability and need to express oneself in visual, graphic form is imperative. However, more important than having the ability to do formal presentation drawings such as full color renderings, designers need to be able to draw informally and rapidly.

In the process of designing, the primary informational input is in the form of rapid successions of mental images. They may be images of the actual surrounding, of spaces yet to be designed, or of details recalled from some past experience. These visual images need to be sifted through the designer's mind. They are evaluated, synthesized, and used in part or whole in the current project or stored for use later in some other situation.

Thus a designer's critical sense — the ability to evaluate functional, aesthetic, cultural, and socioeconomic appropriateness — needs to be constantly refined. Most often, even such other factors as historical references and political impact are points to consider in evaluating and deciding on design solutions.

Drawing is an activity that holds a mystique for most people. Any person doing art work in public becomes an instant curiosity for passersby. Almost all cultures since time immemorial have drawing as an art form. Yet the ability to draw is not universal. There needs to be an affinity for drawing before someone can do it well. Often, there must also be compelling reasons, such as job-related needs, for wanting to draw.

The act of designing is an intensely mental process.

A designer deals with the physical surroundings. Designers work with the natural and man-made elements that make up the environment. Therefore, designers must be aware of the relationship between details and materials, as well as between one object and another. This awareness extends to relationships among spaces within structures, to buildings around them, to towns and cities, to nations and continents. One might even include the relationships among planets, stars, and galaxies. Though not all designs are so universal in scope, no design is an island, existing solely by itself. Directly or indirectly, design affects everyone in the entire world.

It remains a basic tenet that good designers should strive to improve the environment through their efforts.

Since design is such a pervasive activity, the ability to instantaneously make critical judgment is vital. One way to sharpen this skill is through sketching. By definition, a sketch is done rapidly. By not lingering over any point or detail, by making quick

decisions on what to include or what to omit in a sketch, you are refining your ability for taking decisive action. In quickly making an aesthetic judgment, or recognizing some thematic significance while looking at a scene to sketch, you are sharpening your skill in grasping the essence of a situation. Being able to recognize the essence means you can then arrive at solutions that address the core questions of design problems.

Even if you are not directly involved with the design profession, you should be aware of the physical environment: buildings and the spaces within, landscape areas outside and their interrelationships, natural spaces and man-made equipment, particularly automobiles, highways, and all that impact on one another.

The urge to make things is a manifestation of one of mankind's basic needs along with the needs for food and the urge for procreation. Therefore, to take the built environment as the primary subject for sketching is to be involved with a primordial desire. It is a fulfilling and ever varying topic.

This book is organized along the lines I take while sketching. Starting with pictorial subjects, I will point out some of my reasons for selecting certain subjects and scenes for drawing. I will next explain the use of various elements for composing pictures. By telling you how and why I sketch, I hope to give you some insight into the making of pictures.

The third part details the procedures I employ for sketching pictures rapidly, some of the materials and equipment used and the process of drawing in the field as well as in the studio. Felt-tip markers with various types of points are the only drawing instruments used. I will not discuss a lot of other materials. However, what is included will be dealt with in detail.

As designers, there are certain conventions in drawing style which make designer drawings "designerly." Aside from showing some of these mannerisms in the fourth part, I will also encourage you to go beyond stereotypical cliches to achieve a personal manner of expression.

Years of teaching have taught me that a person does not really learn drawing techniques by merely looking at completed pictures. It is more advantageous for a student to see how and, more important, why a drawing was done in that particular way. Obviously, a third party can decipher how a drawing was done by closely examining composition, pen stroke, and so on. It is not so easy (or accurate) to explain why certain subjects were selected, or why certain aspects were omitted, or why elements were placed in their positions, unless they are explained by the artist personally.

Thus I will verbalize my thought process as I point out various features of my own sketches. I believe this will help you, the reader, gain some insight into the creative meaning of sketching.

Rounding out the book will be a portfolio of sketches from many parts of the world where I have traveled through the years.

As much as possible, sketches in this book are reproduced in full scale and in color. This is done so that you can see the characteristics of pen strokes and the layering of colors in actual size. I believe that it is perfectly legitimate for you to lay a piece of paper over my sketches and trace them. This is not done with the idea of mechanically reproducing my sketches, but to familiarize yourself with the flow of the pen and with the control of the medium in applying the felt-tip markers. With practice, you will become familiar with drawing mannerisms and develop your own style.

Above all, drawing should be an enjoyable, relaxing activity. Since sketches, by definition, are done rapidly, little time and expense are involved. If you do not regard each sketch as something terribly sacred or somehow having to be "perfect," you will relax into the drawing activity. This will result in more spontaneous drawings and, at the same time, you will like sketching more.

So, relax, go forth and enjoy!

PICTORIAL SUBJECTS

For a person who is involved with the physical environment, be you an architect, a designer of interior spaces or products, a graphic designer or an artist, being aware of the visual environment is fundamental to peak performance. Drawing what you see around you is one way of becoming intimately familiar with your surroundings. In the process of drawing you have to select the emphasis, highlights, and the aesthetic focus. Since you are not a camera, you cannot mechanically record every detail you see. Therefore, when you draw, every line, color and every detail must go through a process of selection, elimination or critical judgment, using some kind of aesthetic sense. It is the honing of this ability to make critical judgment that is the real value of sketching the visual environment.

What makes an interesting subject to draw? Since you are drawing from real life, all that you see around you and all that you can experience as you move through your day are possible subjects to sketch and record on paper. The act of sketching is the recording of contemporary life as it happens and as you live it firsthand.

There is no lack of subjects to draw. There are the big scenes, such as the panoramic view of Hong Kong harbor in the previous

sketch. The man-made skyline of the city is in a never-ending battle with the natural outline of the mountains in the background. It calls to mind the epic struggles of human-kind trying to control nature and, somehow, not succeeding. Nature can make a grand statement with a simple gesture such as the massive mountains in the sketch, while people fuss with buildings, which only show up the pettiness and egocentric nature of individual human efforts.

If you look more closely, you can examine the physical environment in more detail. The buildings in central Hong Kong are located along winding streets, up, down, and around hillsides, making them face different directions. As they vary in design and in height, the result is a chaotic, vibrant look, giving concrete evidence to this metropolis as the commercial hub of the Orient. The buildings seem to be trying to reach ever higher, to catch a bit of sunshine and fresh air. Like the people who occupy them, these buildings strive to assert some degree of individuality, to be a little different from one another, so as not to be lost in the crowd.

Modern society suffers from excess. There are too many people in too confined spaces, trying to make some sense out of an ever-changing world that is threatening to engulf them. Individual identity is too often limited to the little cubicles to which modern urbanites are consigned. It is a commentary at once of the sad conditions for human beings in the contemporary world and of the undying spirit of individualism, which strives to express itself in the face of deadening conformity.

A designer has to remember to design in context. What you design has an effect on its surroundings and its users. Design is not an isolated endeavor. It is very much an activity that calls for constant dialogue. It is a dialogue between the elements and materials within a design, as well as between the design and its environment. It is a dialogue that is between the users of the design and the designer. By examining the surroundings closely, by putting it down in sketch form, you are establishing a form of dialogue with the environment.

Since you are sketching from reality, you will be surprised at how much diversity and vitality there is in contemporary life, especially in urban life. In a modern society there is an intensity, urbanity, and earthiness that has evolved over time and spans continents. Visual interest and vitality are manifest from the tiered streets of to-day's Hong Kong to the many spires of the still in-use fifteenth-century cathedral of Seville.

In the visual environment, you can find many sorts of contrasting forms. One such contrast is between the rigidly similar coops of new apartments next to the whimsical caricatures of cemetery ornaments.

It is an ironic comparison that people live in look-alike boxes, but are buried in so uniquely individualistic edifices!

To reduce this kind of inconsistency, those involved in shaping the environment have to be vigilantly aware of design priorities. As champions of individual rights, the sophisticated urbanite may speak out for personal expression and the right to divert from the norm. Yet people are increasingly forced to live or work in rigid compartments, on the whole totally indistinguishable one from another, from Europe to Asia, in authoritarian states, and in "free" societies.

Designers are in a position to affect the physical surrounding. They also have a responsibility to make it a better place in which to live, work and play.

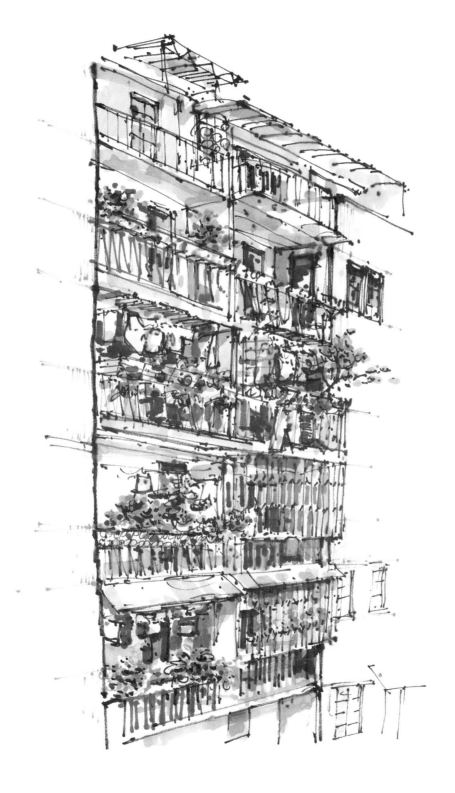

In sketching the architectural environment, you have the opportunity to observe that many designs are inflexible and intolerant of adaptation. Often, cultural idiosyncrasies and users' choices are ignored or dismissed outright by self-centered and insensitive designers.

Here are some balconies at the rear of a nondescript building. All the balconies are built identically, but the tenants have personalized them with grilles and flower boxes of various design. Plants, flowers, and multi-colored laundry hanging out to dry provide some added individuality.

You will become more sensitive to the human condition if you make the effort to observe and record it on paper. As a designer, your sensitivity can help to reach design solutions that will better address some of the problems encountered by people in the modern world.

Contemporary life reflects a sense of dynamism. It is the dynamism of continuous historical evolution, of development and growth, of reaffirmed values. This means that many buildings old and new are continuously adapted, improved upon, and utilized, as exemplified by the juxtaposed rooftops seen from the towers of Chartres cathedral in this sketch.

Even though some of the surfaces are patched and stained, there is no sense of decay or abandonment in the area. There is, instead, the feeling that the buildings are in their rightful places, that they are being used and very much a part of contemporary life, as they must have been for decades, perhaps even for centuries.

The span of centuries is one way time is expressed. Since sketching is essentially a rapid activity occurring over a short period of time, the act of sketching can be used to record time in other ways.

Whether it is a specific moment or a span of days, months, or years, time is an integral element in design consideration. You have to be cognizant of the time period during which your design will function. Obviously, a space designed specifically for day use will be different from one meant to be used only at night. If it is to last for years, a proposed design will have to be projected through various time frames to ascertain viability in changing seasons and changing lighting conditions.

This is a composite view from a fast moving train in northern China. The train was traveling at speed and so the view was continuously changing. This sketch is made up of different views. The central portion with the village was done first, and the hills on the left next. Then those on the right were drawn when the train rounded a corner.

I found this view outside the train interesting: hillsides forming crisscrossing lines that express the kinetic, dynamic quality that is the essence of the scene; the winding river acts as a counter-balance to the diagonal lines of the hills. Since the moving train created a constantly shifting scene, it was not feasible to draw any one view, so I decided to capture segments of the view and made a composite picture.

This sketch uses a few lines in a manner that resembles traditional Chinese brush paintings. Not only is this approach appropriate because the sketch was done in China, but the scene actually looked like that. There were the craggy hills with spare clumps of trees and layers of hills that are so familiar in traditional Chinese landscape paintings.

Seasonal changes create distinct qualities in the atmosphere.

On a cold, snowy day, there was a haze in the air. Colors were muted and bleached. Outlines were softened as if viewed through a filtered lens. This Japanese temple of weathered wood blended into the haze, further enhancing the feeling of starkness and bone-chilling cold.

I happened upon this scene in a deserted park in Tokyo. It was late afternoon and no one had yet walked on the freshly fallen snow. There was a haunting, abandoned feeling. Rather mysterious cavelike recesses in the shaded areas contrasted starkly with the open, exposed coldness of the untrammeled snow. The orange-red railing added the only bright color. It was also the only thin, linear element in a composition of broad masses.

Fast changing scenery and dynamic qualities are valid subjects for sketching, as are more static views. At low tide in the mud flats of the Pearl River estuary in southern China, dwarf trees stuck out of the mud as if they were artificially inserted. The scene had a surrealistic overtone.

These sketches involve the passage of time as much as glimpses drawn from a moving train or a ferryboat, for tides and morning mist come and go. It is the very spontaneity of sketching that is best suited to capture these moments.

Dusk is an interesting time for drawing, because it is a time of change: the ending of the day's events and the beginning of night. Pausing to sketch at this time is a reflective activity. It allows one to catch one's breath, to take stock and be introspective.

Lengthening shadows under overhanging trees create a dramatic envelope, embracing people going home from work in this street in China. The atmosphere is charged with a subdued deliberateness. People are cycling in one direction, heads down, intent on going home. Low hanging branches, deep shadows, and the narrow street combine to create an intimacy and a personal scale — qualities often missing in thoroughfares designed for motorized traffic.

The quality of light is a very important criterion in the design process. Light changes constantly from hour to hour, day to day, season to season. Indeed, light changes from location to location, whether it is a distance of a few feet or a separation continents wide. Even on the same site, the quality of light varies from one side to another.

In a late summer afternoon that seemed to linger on, a soft blue sky and deepening shadows dominated the Spanish city of Granada. This sketch depicts the northwest corner of the main cathedral. There was a warm glow on the sunny side of the building. At the same time, there were cool shadows on the side away from the sun. Details and surface textures were muted by the soft lighting at that time of the day.

Since color is perceived through light, the quality of light will affect the colors of a design. Whether you are working in artificial lighting, natural light, or some combination of both, ambient lighting is crucial to color selection in your design. So be especially conscious of the type of lighting in which your design will be seen.

29

Pictorial elements across the surface of a picture also interact with one another two-dimensionally. In this sketch of a bonsai plant, the background becomes the voids or negative spaces among the branches and leaf groupings. Negative spaces give substance to the forms of the positive elements. In this case, they give the latter a light, lacy and airy appearance.

The ability to analyze the physical appearance of objects in the environment is a great asset to a designer. Notice that some objects are light and airy, while others are the opposite. The rocks on the seashore in the next picture evoke a massive, strong, and solid imagery.

When I begin a sketch, I try to place the major elements within an imaginary frame, usually rectangular in shape. Thus I am thinking about composition and selecting pictorial elements at the same time. I will discuss composition further in the next chapter, but I wish to point out here that pictorial composition comes early in the creation of a sketch.

When you are composing a picture, try to express the major elements in bold gestural strokes. Use them to establish the orientation or directional movement of the drawing.

A dramatic foreground to background relationship creates distance and movement. Not much of the cliff-side in the foreground is shown in this sketch. Still, the perspective angle is such that one gets the feeling of standing on the edge of the cliff, about to teeter and fall.

While one usually looks up to a mountain from below, this is a view of flat fields as seen from a higher altitude. It makes this sketch somewhat unusual, with a startling quality in its visual impact.

I have been trying to point out that to a designer subjects of interest exist all around, in natural areas as well as in the built environment. As you pick out subjects for sketching, keep in mind that sketching is a means to improve your evaluative and critical skills. A sketch is not an end in itself. It is not a design solution of any sort. It is merely an expression of your sensitivity to the visual world.

COMPOSITION

Composition is the positioning of various elements in a picture field. Such elements as lines and forms are placed in ways so as to result in interesting pictures. One purpose of composition is to attract and hold a viewer's attention. By manipulating pictorial elements, a viewer is guided around the picture field, lingering here and there to savor various meaningful nuances.

In thinking about composition, the visual world may be looked upon as being made up of basic shapes or forms: squares, rectangles, triangles, or ovals. Look at the direction an object takes. A columnar tree or a tall building tends to divide a scene vertically. The sides of a triangular object, such as a mountainside, may slash diagonally across a picture field. In other words, what you see around you are objects that can be regarded in terms of basic design shapes.

A series of vertical elements are used in this sketch that divides the picture field into narrow segments. When a number of identical or nearly identical shapes are present, they set up a tempo or pace for the composition. Here, vertical forms march across the picture field in a natural, organic way. The slight differences among the trees exude a sense of the breeziness and liveliness of the scene, contrasting greatly with the rigidly structured size and shape of the columns in the next sketch.

The immediate reaction to this picture is that of looking at a sketch depicting man-made objects, since the major elements (the columns) are unequivocally artificial. They are uniform in size, shape, and equally red in color. However, this picture is not dull or static, because the vivid red color brings out a sense of gaiety and is as playful as the swaying palms of the previous picture.

Compositionally speaking, the major difference between these two pictures is that in the last picture the elements exist two-dimensionally across the page, while here the columns bring out depth in three-dimensional perspective. By varying the scale of the columns, a front to back movement is created.

Negative space delineates positive space. We see by sensing the contrast (in value, color, texture, etc.) between an object and the space around it. Without the differentiation, it would be like being in a pitch-dark room, unable to distinguish one object from another. Space around an object is needed to set objects apart.

In order to create a successful composition, the artist strives for balance, harmony, and variety among pictorial elements. Facing a particular scene that you, as an artist, find interesting, you must evaluate critically and choose selectively in your decision about what to include in your picture.

When you begin a sketch, do not set out to draw individual objects. A tree, for example, is not an isolated object standing alone, even if it is the only tree around. It should be regarded as a vertical element when compared with the horizontal ground under it. It may be oval, triangular, or columnar in shape. A tree may be tall and thin, or relatively low and fat. It may be open and lacy, solid and massive, or clumpy with skeletal lines (branches and trunk) showing through. Draw the form and its structure, but do not literally or mechanically draw the object itself.

One of the fundamental design elements is linearity, or the line form. An object or scene can be expressed by its linearity when it resembles a line in its proportions. A tall, thin object is linear vertically while the horizon on an empty sea can be expressed by a horizontal line.

In a pictorial composition, such lines can be used to divide the picture field into areas with interesting proportional relationships.

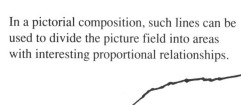

Lines have direction that can be used to point to or guide a viewer around various parts of a picture.

Lines have characteristics. They are "hard" when they are straight, especially when they are long and heavy. Lines are soft and organic when they are curved.

It was springtime in southern China and the leaves were young and tender, giving the tree in the center a delicate, lacy appearance, which is enhanced by a plain, flat background. The tree also contrasted sharply with the hard, straight lines of the roof edges and balcony railing. Notice that strong, straight lines point to the center, forcing it to be the focal area of the picture.

Balance does not necessarily mean symmetry. In pictorial composition, dead symmetry is usually avoided, because it brings about a static and dull composition. It is generally more interesting to balance elements by deliberately placing them off-center so that a larger, heavier group of elements can be counter balanced by a smaller one.

What struck me about this scene was the good opportunity to play up the contrast among the elements. The trees, tower, and terrace in the foreground were dark and heavy visually. Together they form a tray at the base of the composition. The tall trees and tower can be compared to handles of the tray, supporting the lighter element, which is the sun drenched hill in the background. This is one example of how more than one major element can be used in a picture.

It was said earlier that a picture should not be split down the middle, as this would produce an uninteresting composition. Since rules are meant to be broken, or at least bent, the next two figures use very strong vertical elements almost right down the center of the composition.

Although the vertical is the dominant element, the horizontal acts as a cap on top to level out the composition. Thus the viewer uses a sweeping movement of the eye in taking in the picture.

By being aware of contrasts in the environment, designers and artists can sharpen their ability to observe.

These two pictures have a combination of vertical and horizontal elements. The subjects were fascinating because of the dark shadow areas. In the strong Andalusian sun, these shadow areas created chasms at once mysterious and powerful visually.

Notice, however, that this is not a true symmetrical split, which would have been dull and static. The dark element is an organic shape, pulsating on a slant down the middle, but not the dead center, of the picture. There is a leaning toward the upper right side, but the eye is drawn to the upper left by the perspective angle of the building.

Thus a viewer is taken on a deliberately guided tour of the picture field.

A rather difficult subject to draw, the space is the interior of the Catholic cathedral (which was built as a Muslim mosque) in Cordoba, Spain. Much of the interior is dark. A forest of red and yellow arches are variously lit by small skylights that appear to be randomly placed. Bright shafts of sunlight cut deeply into the space, highlighting niches containing chapels and altars.

The compositional device used here takes advantage of strong vertical elements to frame the picture at the sides. The arches are seen as rounded caps at the top of the picture. The high dark/light value contrast anchors the bottom. Highlights occur in the complementary color contrast between the blue-black of the shadows and the yellow-gold of the altar.

The windows and doors of this restaurant were boarded up with different materials, making the scene a composition of flat surfaces in various colors and textures. **Colors can be viewed in masses that can then be used as elements for balance, focus, or emphasis.**

Contrasting colors, those on a complementary scale or highly different on the value scale, can also create tension or a sense of agitation and busyness, while analogous colors seem more serene and calm. You must be aware of the dynamic qualities of colors so that colors can be used to your advantage in composing pictures.

TENSION

DENSE

OPEN

DARK

LIGHT

TENSION

Elements can be grouped in different densities, resulting in different visual weights. Denser groups weigh more heavily than the more open, loosely organized ones. Thus you can compose a picture using contrasting values to create tension between elements, to visually emphasize certain areas or to articulate spaces.

Negative space can be used to establish visual relationships among the elements of a drawing. When objects are closely placed, there is a tension between them. When the objects are farther apart, the space between them flows more slowly and easily, thus reducing tension and speed. This kind of manipulation is often called articulation.

Since the purpose of composition is to guide a viewer around a picture, sometimes a minimal hint is all that is needed to suggest a picture, allowing the viewer to fill in the rest of the scene. It is important that you find the one detail that suggests the essence of the picture: the one item that will pique the imagination of the viewer such that he or she will go on to fill in the rest of the picture without being shown every detail.

By emphasizing one area, more details can be developed and the essence of a picture can be stressed.

In the previous sketch, the essential thing is to show life in a city such as Granada. By highlighting the major street, more details such as selected storefronts, street traffic, and various facades can be emphasized.

By not showing an entire scene, thus suggesting that there are things beyond the bend in a path, or around a corner, a picture can possess a mystical feeling that goes past the physical boundaries of the drawing.

A note here about the importance of negative space:

A negative space must never be thought of as unused or as a leftover area or that somehow only the positive items have pictorial meaning. Keep in mind that all parts of the picture field make up a composition, whether they contain positive elements or negative space.

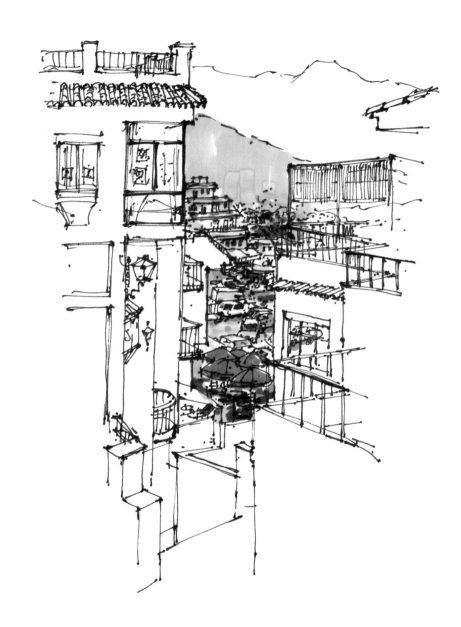

A compositional device similar to the ones used in the previous pages is seen here. Long, straight lines are used to contrast with short, more organic lines in the focal area.

This sketch brings out a dilemma increasingly found by contemporary designers in urban settings. The problem they face is that often there are many tall buildings grouped so closely together that what would have been a panoramic view is reduced to narrow slices of scenery between buildings. For what purpose are floor to ceiling windows used in high-rise structures?

This view was drawn from a downtown hotel window. Since the central area is sufficiently complex to hold a viewer's attention, only this core was fully rendered in detail.

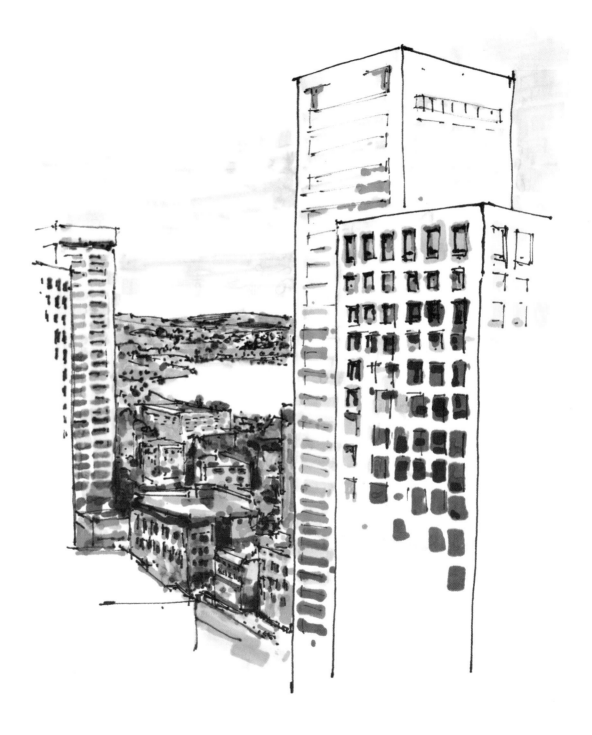

Frequently seen in architectural renderings, especially in student work, is the use of a large circle scribed around the middle of a picture with only the area within the circle colored. This is a boring and mechanical device. Anyone can use it without regarding the nature of the scene being drawn. The circumscribed circle mechanically defines the focus of the picture. Using this method, the subject, degree of complexity, or character of the space all do not matter.

Allowing the inherent nature of the elements in a scene to highlight a focal area is much more natural. The intrinsic character of the space should be used to define a sketch.

Here, the morning sun casts strong shadows on the one visibly wider street leading to the church and grouping of larger buildings. It is not necessary to color in more than this street and the major buildings because they are the dominant elements in the scene.

The brightest colors are the red roofs spotted on the right side of the picture. These create an imbalance of color, which is ordinarily not acceptable in pictorial composition. In this case, however, the red areas form a vertical line that is balanced by the darker, cooler horizontal line formed by the larger buildings on the left. The viewer is thus led into and around the picture by the red spots and the slash of colors.

Composition, therefore, is more than merely placing elements around a picture.

The composition of a picture should complement the nature of the objects and scene being depicted. It should highlight the strong points and subjugate the lesser or distracting elements. Above all, a well-composed picture takes a viewer on a carefully guided tour all around the picture.

SKETCHING MECHANICS

By definition, a sketch is a drawing executed in a rapid manner within a short time. The desirable characteristics of a sketch are its spontaneous look, its freshness, liveliness, and, most often, an unfinished quality that seems to promise further growth and development. A good sketch is never overworked. Its colors and pen strokes are laid down with a deliberate firmness that is never heavy-handed. A sketch artist, in capturing the essence of a scene with a few strokes of the pen, is exercising value judgment and expressing an aesthetic statement. Unlike a photograph, a sketch cannot depict all the minute physical details a good camera lens can. On the other hand, an artist can selectively remove or insert elements that are not actually there in the scene to compose a better picture. A good sketch captures enough detail to invoke the sense of a scene and lets the imagination fill in the gaps.

For both the viewer and the artist, the comprehension of the essence of a sketch occurs within a short time. To appreciate the sense of what is being viewed, the artist needs to work fast and decisively. There must not be a dawdling over unessential details, or clouding the central theme with unnecessary embellishments. This means that the artist has to possess a keen value judgment to be able to focus readily on the essential qualities of the scene being drawn.

To practice working within a strict time limit, I have imposed upon myself a period of roughly thirty minutes, within which I must complete a sketch or retrace the drawing time and time again, until I have become so familiar with the sketch that I can complete it within the half-hour period.

This is strictly an arbitrary time period and you may find that you wish to start with a longer time frame until you are familiar with the method.

There are reasons for restricting oneself in this way. Beginners, and students especially, tend to regard each and every drawing they create as precious. Perhaps this is due to the limited output at their particular stage of development, but it should be kept in mind that a sketch is transitional.

A sketch is a means, not the end. So use it to develop dexterity with the medium, to visualize in three dimensions, to become conscious of the interplay of colors, values, and the textural qualities of objects in the environment. A sketch is a means of refining one's sense of aesthetics to cut through superficial details to arrive at the essence. Do not regard a sketch as a definitive or ultimate statement. Rather, if you consider a sketch as a tool to better understand your environment, you will be more at ease with your drawings and will draw with more facility and authority.

If you are a beginner or not very experienced, it is perfectly understandable that you would feel some reluctance to draw in public. Trying to concentrate while strangers are looking over your shoulders is an unnerving experience. Think not of them as critics. Most people are there not to judge your abilities. Most people look with a sense of awe and admiration at how anyone could transfer on paper what they see in front of them. Some form of visual representation of real life objects and scenes is found in almost all cultures, but not everyone is endowed with a natural ability to draw. It has to be nurtured and developed by an affinity for drawing and a perseverance to continue practicing. The more you draw, the better you become, and the more at ease you will be with sketching in public.

I begin a picture by drawing a base sketch. It is placed under my drawing paper, through which the base sketch can be seen to act as a guide for the actual drawing. The base sketch is drawn on tracing paper with rapid pen strokes, taking no more than a minute or two to complete. Use only the lines needed to block out and locate the main elements of the picture.

With the base sketch as a guide, I am freed from worrying about composition. Most of the variables are decided upon in this early part of the process. The placement of elements, light sources, proportional balance, perspective lines, and so on, are all considered and in place. I do not have to guess at what next to draw or if the picture will balance.

Thus I can freely range throughout the picture field, applying pen strokes to bring out shapes and forms, shadows and high lights. Most of all, since I do not have to worry about details, this process lets me work rapidly to achieve the spontaneous quality of a sketch.

SKETCH DEMONSTRATION #1

COLORS USED ON THIS PAGE:

WARM GREY 4
WARM GREY 5
WARM GREY 7

**WORK ON LARGE, ARCHITEC-
TURAL SURFACES FIRST.**

**START WITH MEDIUM GREY IN A
SHADOW AREA. YOU CAN ALWAYS
DARKEN, BUT IT IS DIFFICULT TO
LIGHTEN A COLOR, SINCE THE
MARKERS ARE IN INDELIBLE INK.**

NOTE SOURCE OF LIGHT.

**PEN STROKES REFLECT DIRECTION
AND CHARACTER OF SURFACES.**

**THIN,
VERTICAL
SURFACE.**

**HORIZONTAL BAND OF WALL
SURFACE.**

**FIRST DELINEATE
SHADOW AREAS.**

LEAVE HIGHLIGHTS BLANK.

**PAINT EACH VISIBLE SURFACE
SEPARATELY. FIRST COLOR ONE
SURFACE, LET IT DRY BY GOING
ON TO ANOTHER PART OF THE
SKETCH BEFORE RETURNING TO
WORK ON ADJACENT SURFACES.**

**PAINT AROUND OBJECTS. USE
CONTRAST TO DELINEATE, BUT DO
NOT ACTUALLY OUTLINE OBJECTS
(NOT YET).**

59

BASIC COLORS LAID DOWN IN VARYING DEGREES AND INTENSITIES.

ENRICH SURFACES WITH LAYERED COLORS.

ADDITIONAL COLORS USED ON THIS PAGE:

RED BROWN 1
BEIGE
MAUVE

VARY COLORS AND VALUES FROM TOP TO BOTTOM AND FROM FRONT TO BACK. RICHER AND DARKER AT THE FRONT AND TOP; MORE FADED AND LIGHTER AS SURFACE RECEDES.

WORK THROUGHOUT THE PICTURE. DO NOT TRY TO FINISH ANY ONE AREA AT ONE TIME.

PAINT EACH SURFACE SEPARATELY.

OVERLAP COLORS
AND LAYERS.

DO NOT DRAW HEAVY HANDEDLY.
MARKERS SHOULD CONTACT
PAPER LIGHTLY.

LEAVE HIGHLIGHTED
AREAS WHITE.

ADDITIONAL COLORS USED
ON THIS PAGE:

WARM GREY 6 (FINE LINE)
GREY 6 (FINE LINE)
GREY 8
GREEN ORANGE GREEN
RAW WOOD

BUILD UP CAST SHADOWS.

FLOORING INDICATED WITH
HORIZONTAL PEN STROKES.

BEGIN DELINEATING OUTLINES BY
EMPHASIZING SHADED SIDES.

WORK RAPIDLY; DO NOT DAWDLE.

61

ADDITIONAL COLORS USED ON
THIS PAGE:

CHROME YELLOW
BLUE BLACK
PALE WALNUT
RED BROWN

KEEP HEEL OF HAND OFF THE
PAPER. KEEP WRIST RIGID. PIVOT
ARM AT ELBOW.

ENRICH SURFACES
WITH STRONG
ACCENT COLORS.

KEEP LIGHT SOURCE
IN MIND.

USE PROGRESSIVELY DARKER,
BRIGHTER AND RICHER COLORS
AS YOU GO FROM STEP TO STEP.

62

ADDITIONAL COLORS USED
ON THIS PAGE:

WARM GREY 0
BLACK (ULTRAFINE LINE)
BLACK (FINE LINE)

DO NOT MECHANICALLY
OUTLINE EVERY EDGE.
SHARPEN OBJECTS BY
SELECTIVE USE OF
OUTLINES.

ENHANCE DIMENSIONAL
CHARACTER BY LIGHT
AND HEAVY OUTLINES.

Remember that the base sketch is only a guide. Use it to compose your picture. It has taken very little time to draw the base sketch, so do not regard it as being precious or inviolate. Learn to be flexible and feel as you draw. If you have made too many corrections and the base sketch becomes hard to read, put another sheet of paper over it and retrace your sketch, using the correct lines and making any further adjustments.

A base sketch may be rather detailed. As you become more proficient, you will need less details in the base sketch to guide you.

You will also find that drawing on site requires fewer guidelines, since you can readily see all the details. Also, you are often pressed for time. On the other hand, do not dawdle over the base sketch even if you have the time, for dawdling tends to inhibit spontaneity and freshness.

A rough sketch of a shopping mall. The space was visually overwhelming. Multilevels criss-crossed and variously patterned materials abounded. There were numerous shiny metallic and reflective surfaces. All this busyness and visual activity makes it a natural scene for a quick sketch.

The base sketch was done on Aquabee 638 paper, which has a tendency to absorb maker colors and make them "bleed." While this characteristic is especially nice for sketching organic subjects, it is not in keeping with the machine-made materials of this scene.

The finished sketch was done on Aquabee 633 paper. It is less absorbent, resulting in sharper lines reflective of the nature of this subject.

Aquabee 638:

Plastic coated on reverse side, non-seep through.
Porous, similar to ricepaper.
For landscapes and pictures of organic forms.
"Bleeding" effect resembles watercolors.

PAPER as manufactured by the **Bee Paper Co., Passaic, NJ.**

Aquabee 633:

Treated paper, no seepage of colors.
Less absorbent than #638 paper: drawn lines appear sharper, crisper; colors blend and layer more distinctly.
For drawing man-made objects and surfaces.
Good for close parallel-line shading.

Drawing Pads:

9"x12" tracing paper and marker paper pads

Basic set of markers:

A few warm and cool greys, neutral greens, accent colors, and the black markers.

LIST OF MARKERS

209-L0	WARM GREY 0		273-L	PALE WALNUT
209-L2	WARM GREY 2		283-L	RAW WOOD
209-L3	WARM GREY 3		293-L	BROWN
209-L4	WARM GREY 4		383-L	NATURAL OAK
209-L5	WARM GREY 5		402-L	CHROME YELLOW
209-L5F	WARM GREY 5		423-L	BEIGE
209-L6	WARM GREY 6		426-L	RUST
209-L7	WARM GREY 7		433-L	BUFF
209-L8	WARM GREY 8		434-L	MAUVE
209-L9	WARM GREY 9		436-L	MELON RED
229-L1	GREY 1		306-L	RED RED VIOLET
229-L2	GREY 2		226-L	RED ORANGE
229-L3	GREY 3		214-L	VIOLET RED VIOLET
229-L4	GREY 4		205-L9	BLUE GREEN 9
229-L5	GREY 5		265-L0	BLUE 0
229-L6	GREY 6		265-L1	BLUE 1
229-L6F	GREY 6		365-L	BLUE BLACK
229-L7	GREY 7		365-LF	BLUE BLACK
229-L8	GREY 8		415-L	COBALT
229-L9	GREY 9		488-L	PALE IVY
229-L	BLACK		478-L	WILLOW
229-LF	BLACK		448-L	APPLE GREEN
229-LU	BLACK		428-L	MOSS
311	COLORLESS BLENDER		258-L9	GREEN 9
213-L0	RED BROWN 0		248-L	GREEN ORANGE GREEN
213-L1	RED BROWN 1		248-LU	GREEN ORANGE GREEN
213-L	RED BROWN		248-L9	GREEN ORANGE GREEN 9
233-L	YELLOW BROWN		208	YELLOW GREEN

These markers come in three types of nibs:

1. The regular chisel-shaped nibs.
   Labeled as xxx-L.

These produce different types of lines depending on whether you use the broad side, the narrow side, or the tip.

2. The Fine nib.
   Labeled as xxx-LF.

3. The Ultrafine nib.
   Labeled as xxx-LU.

All marker names and numbers are as used in the **Design Art Markers** series by **Eberhard Faber** and distributed by **Faber-Castell, Lewisburg, TN.**

This collection consists of markers with colors in the major color groups. You may find that you need to augment it to include colors you like better.

The selection of markers and papers is purposely limited in the belief that it is better to focus on a restricted range of materials and learn to use them well, than it is to dabble with a wide range of choices.

Main compartment large enough to hold two 9"x12" drawing pads, camera and lenses, and a basic set of markers.

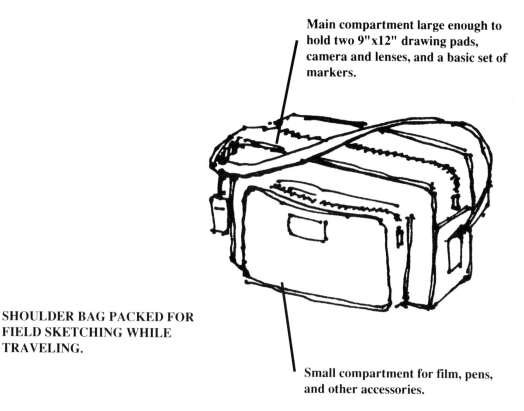

SHOULDER BAG PACKED FOR FIELD SKETCHING WHILE TRAVELING.

Small compartment for film, pens, and other accessories.

If you are on an extended trip, other necessities such as guide books, maps, and personal belongings will find their way into the bag. Take out unneeded items each day before leaving to see the sights. Try to keep the bag as light as possible, because you will feel the weight on your shoulders after carrying it for just a short while.

I find it essential to have some good, basic camera equipment. It is not necessary to be loaded down with rarely used, fancy gadgets. A good 35 mm single-lens reflex camera is essential. I favor a fairly wide 35 mm lens over a "normal" 50 mm lens, because the wider angle lens includes a broader segment of subject matter. To me, it is more representative of natural vision. The 35 mm lens shows more peripheral vision, as my eyes naturally do. It is especially useful for recording architectural interiors.

Color transparency, or slide, film is used to enable the projection of images onto a large screen or wall. Generally, I would keep to a low to medium speed film. They provide richer, warmer colors and finer resolution than films with higher speeds. I always leave an ultraviolet light (UV) filter on the lens to filter out excess ultraviolet light from the sun and to protect the lens itself.

A word here about taking film, exposed or unexposed, through airport security checks. I have never found it to be a problem. To begin with, I do not use lead-lined film pouches. You will really feel their weight if you carry them around in your shoulder bag awhile. Besides, they raise the suspicion of security guards and usually cause more delays. I have gone through as many as ten airport security checks on a single trip with my film in my shoulder bag and have not noticed any fogging. I must quickly add that I use only Kodak films and I cannot attest to films of other makes. In most airports, the security X-ray machines are safe for films. Where they are not safe, warning signs should be present. When you are unsure, such as in obscure airports, it is best to have your film handchecked. For this reason, it is more convenient to have your film, exposed and unexposed, in separate bags, so that you can readily take them out for manual inspection.

It is often difficult to do any sketching in the field at all, especially if you are a traveler in strange places. Usually you are on a tight schedule and there are too many new sights bombarding you from all directions. Everything you see is new and unfamiliar. Under these circumstances, it is difficult to filter out the extraneous or to focus on the essence of a scene for a sketch.

Hence, I find it advantageous to take slides of possible sketch subjects or scenes for later elaboration in the studio. I also find it helpful to make a few verbal and visual notes on a rough outline sketch. Back at the studio, I will project a slide to approximately life-size and, referring to my notes, sketch a scene while recalling sensations of being back at the site.

A photographic slide is better than a print, of course, since you can project it to a larger size for looking at details and for a better feel of the subject. It is true, however, that a slide does not take the place of drawing in a real-life setting. The camera lens does distort and limit the scope of an image. Depending on the camera equipment, your photographic skills and those who process your film, color rendition can often be grossly distorted. Nevertheless, if you have experienced a scene personally, if you have taken the slides yourself, and if you have notes made at the site, sketching later through slides is an alternative to drawing in situ. It certainly expands your scope of subject matters, since now you can take lots of slides, and draw at your leisure after you return home.

Remember, it is important that you, yourself, examine the scene, take the photographs, and make notes at the site. Then, you are more likely to recapture the sensation of being on the site when you sketch in your studio. Also, remember that the idea is not to copy in clinical or photographic detail in your sketches, but to capture the scene's essential feeling.

35 MM COLOR TRANSPARENCY (SLIDE) FILM

KODAK EKTACHROME 100 TO 400 FILM. Results in slightly bluish, cooler colors.
KODAK KODACHROME 64 FILM. Results in warmer, reddish tones.

35 MM SINGLE LENS REFLEX (SLR) CAMERA BODY
Through the lens metering couples exposure time and lens aperture for correct shooting setting for most average photographs. It is better that you learn to adjust settings manually, so that you can control settings for special exposures. The Auto-focus feature is **NBNE***

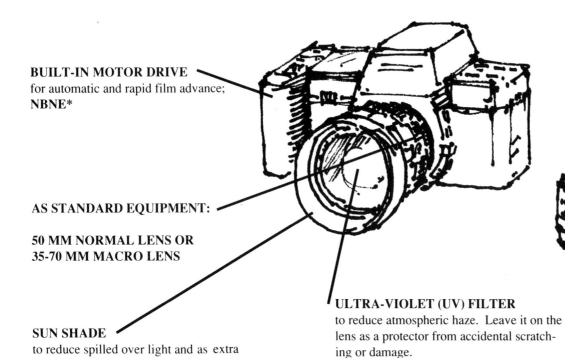

BUILT-IN MOTOR DRIVE
for automatic and rapid film advance; **NBNE***

AS STANDARD EQUIPMENT:

50 MM NORMAL LENS OR 35-70 MM MACRO LENS

SUN SHADE
to reduce spilled over light and as extra protection for lens and filter.

ULTRA-VIOLET (UV) FILTER
to reduce atmospheric haze. Leave it on the lens as a protector from accidental scratching or damage.

70-210 MM MACRO ZOOM LENS

28 or 35 MM WIDE ANGLE LENS

NBNE* extras to have. I also rely heavily on a 35 mm perspective-control lens, with which I can compensate for tilting perspective planes.

*NBNE: NICE BUT NOT ESSENTIAL.

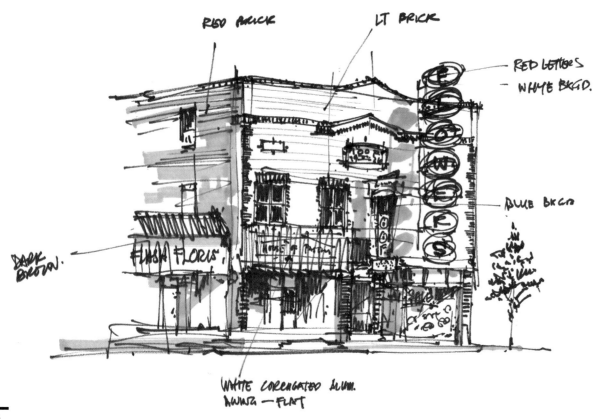

RED BRICK

LT BRICK

RED LETTERS
- WHITE BKGD.

BLUE BKGD

DARK BROWN.

FLASH FLORIS

WHITE CORREGATED ALUM.
AWNG — FLAT

DRAWING IN THE STUDIO

As far as I can remember, I have always been drawing; especially vivid are memories of pictures on the margins of school books. I have doodled and drawn what I could see in my immediate environment, thus honing my ability to observe and translate from mental images into pictures on paper. I remember observing the changing shapes of airplanes as they flew directly away from me and I remember recording them on paper. I must have been in the first grade then. My teachers passed those drawings around, commenting on my cognizance of foreshortening.

Having had an early interest in architecture, my natural inclination is to draw the physical environment, man-made and natural. Formal training in architecture and design reinforces such a tendency. And military training in still photography ensures that I view my world in a freeze-frame compositional format.

Interest since childhood and prior training may be helpful, but the one ingredient absolutely essential to being able to sketch well is the affinity for drawing. If you like to draw, you are naturally inclined to draw, and the more you draw, the more proficient you become. Practice, practice, and practice: there is no way around it. If you like drawing, practicing is not a drudgery but an enjoyable experience, as sketching should be.

There are certain differences between sketching from life in the field and drawing in your own studio. The studio is a more controlled environment, the surroundings and equipment are familiar, ambient lighting and creature comforts are more favorable. Most of all, you have the time and solitude to concentrate on your sketches.

SKETCH DEMONSTRATION #2

IN THIS VIEW OF THE ILE DE ST.
LOUIS IN PARIS, THERE ARE MANY
ORDERED AND REPETITIOUS
ARCHITECTURAL DETAILS. TO
SHOW THEM EFFECTIVELY, THEY
NEED TO BE DEFINITIVELY PLACED
IN THE SKETCH. THEREFORE, THE
BASE SKETCH HAS TO BE WELL
STRUCTURED AND DETAILED.

BASE SKETCH.
DRAWN ON TRACING PAPER.

FOR THIS SKETCH, ONLY THE
BLACK ULTRAFINE, FINE, AND
REGULAR NIBS ARE USED.

AQUABEE #633 PAPER IS USED
BECAUSE OF THE NEED FOR SHARP
LINES AND DETAILS.

BEGIN WITH THE FINE LINE NIB.
THIS PARTICULAR MARKER IS
SOMEWHAT WORN AND DRY,
RESULTING IN SCRATCHY, FUZZY
LINES.

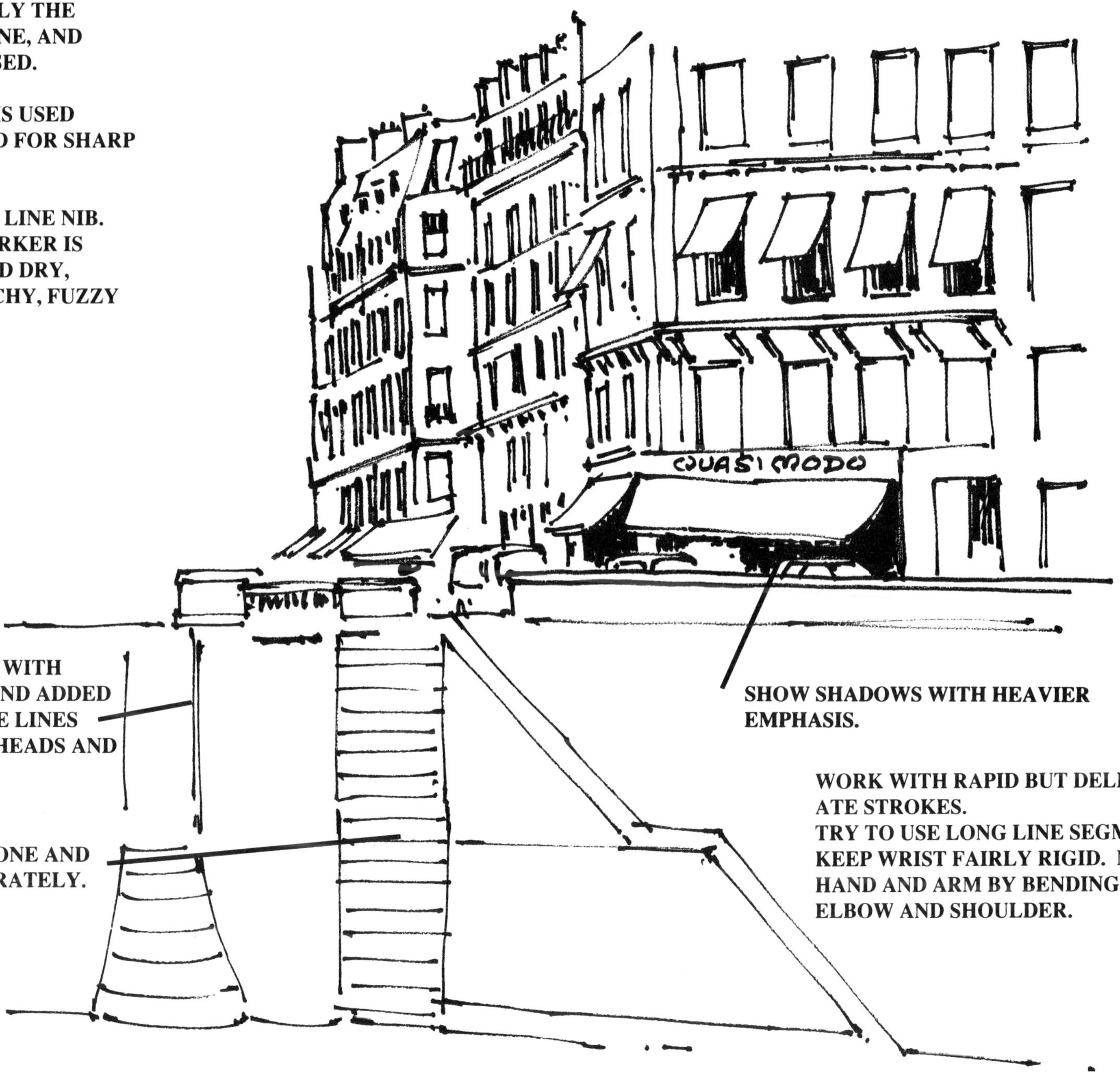

BEGIN AND END LINES WITH
SLIGHT HESITATION AND ADDED
PRESSURE TO ACHIEVE LINES
WITH ACCENTUATED HEADS AND
TAILS.

DRAW INDIVIDUAL STONE AND
BRICK COURSES SEPARATELY.

SHOW SHADOWS WITH HEAVIER
EMPHASIS.

WORK WITH RAPID BUT DELIBER-
ATE STROKES.
TRY TO USE LONG LINE SEGMENTS.
KEEP WRIST FAIRLY RIGID. MOVE
HAND AND ARM BY BENDING AT
ELBOW AND SHOULDER.

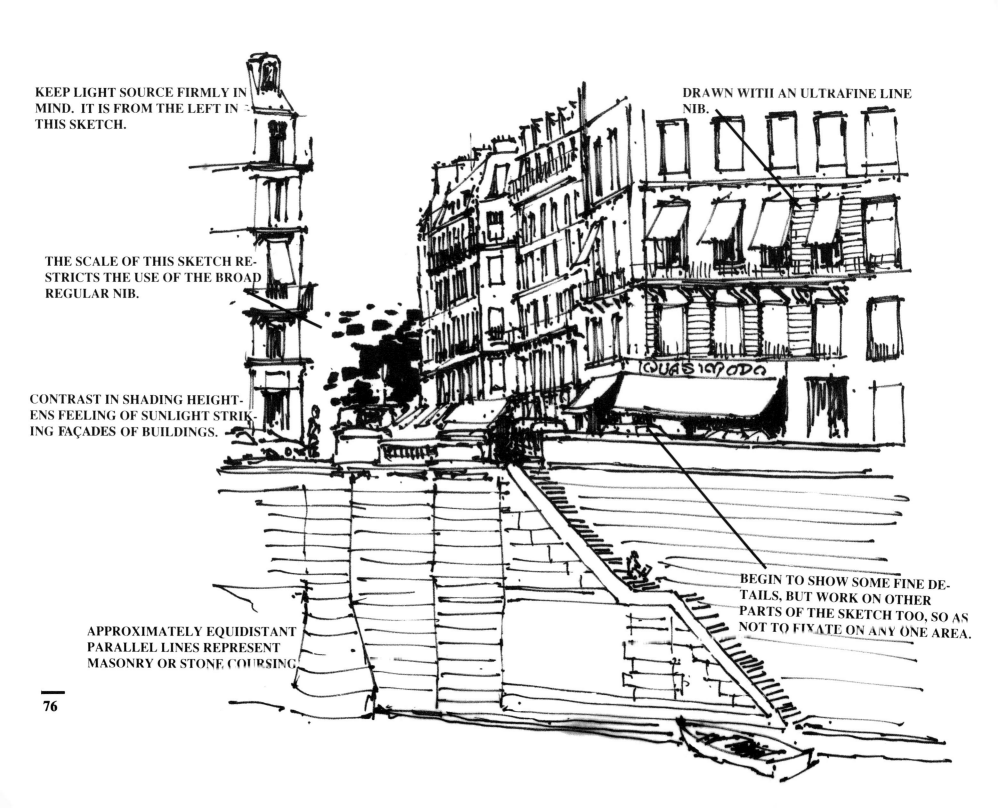

KEEP LIGHT SOURCE FIRMLY IN MIND. IT IS FROM THE LEFT IN THIS SKETCH.

DRAWN WITH AN ULTRAFINE LINE NIB.

THE SCALE OF THIS SKETCH RESTRICTS THE USE OF THE BROAD REGULAR NIB.

CONTRAST IN SHADING HEIGHTENS FEELING OF SUNLIGHT STRIKING FAÇADES OF BUILDINGS.

BEGIN TO SHOW SOME FINE DETAILS, BUT WORK ON OTHER PARTS OF THE SKETCH TOO, SO AS NOT TO FIXATE ON ANY ONE AREA.

APPROXIMATELY EQUIDISTANT PARALLEL LINES REPRESENT MASONRY OR STONE COURSING.

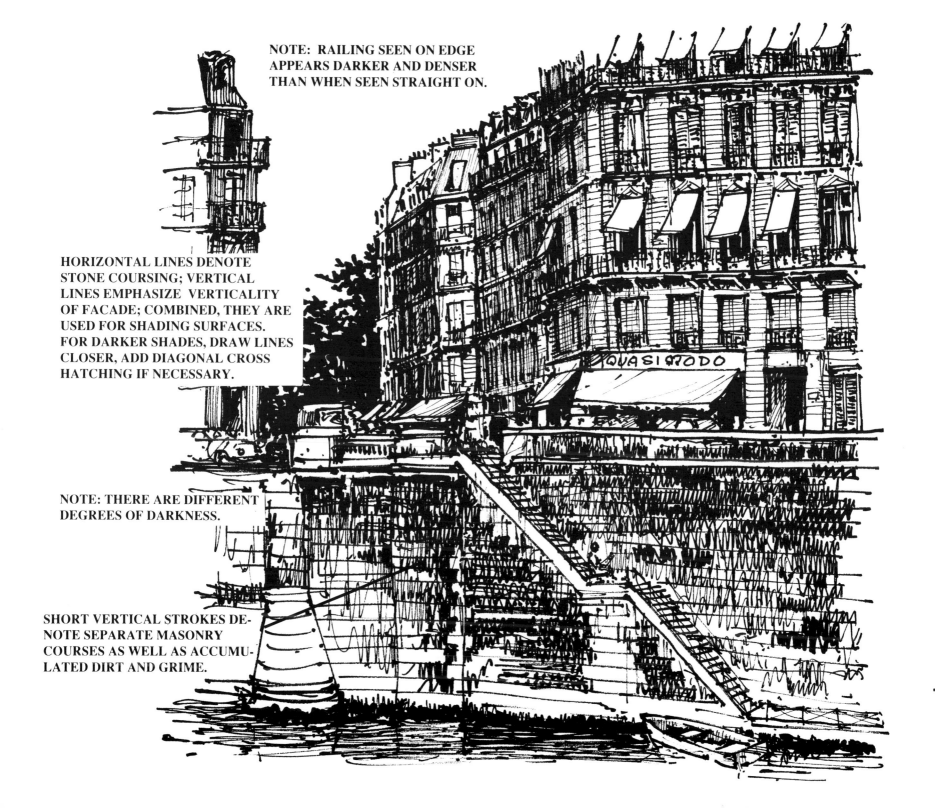

NOTE: RAILING SEEN ON EDGE
APPEARS DARKER AND DENSER
THAN WHEN SEEN STRAIGHT ON.

HORIZONTAL LINES DENOTE
STONE COURSING; VERTICAL
LINES EMPHASIZE VERTICALITY
OF FACADE; COMBINED, THEY ARE
USED FOR SHADING SURFACES.
FOR DARKER SHADES, DRAW LINES
CLOSER, ADD DIAGONAL CROSS
HATCHING IF NECESSARY.

NOTE: THERE ARE DIFFERENT
DEGREES OF DARKNESS.

SHORT VERTICAL STROKES DE-
NOTE SEPARATE MASONRY
COURSES AS WELL AS ACCUMU-
LATED DIRT AND GRIME.

ON-SITE SKETCHING

Sketching in public is a conspicuous act. No matter how you may try to be inconspicuous, you will attract curious onlookers within a few minutes of bringing out your pad and pen. Since you cannot avoid it, you may as well get used to the idea of people looking over your shoulders at your artistic endeavors.

No matter how insecure you feel about your capabilities, it is useful to keep in mind that artistic abilities are rather nebulous qualities. There are "good" and "bad" artists, to be sure, but it is more important to remember that there are always "better" and "worse" artists than oneself. The very fact that you are drawing means you have abilities not common to most people. It means you are trying to improve yourself, which makes you potentially a better artist.

I remember a day in south China, where I had done some sketches among the oddly shaped karst hills so characteristically shown in Chinese landscape paintings. Upon returning to the hotel, I sought out a secluded verandah railing and became absorbed in putting some finishing touches on a sketch. The first time I looked up from my pad, there was a whole ring of faces around me, silently and intently watching. I nodded and smiled, but the faces remained impassive and unmoving. So I continued drawing. After a few minutes, I held the sketch out at arm's length and said, in Chinese: "Not very good, eh?" Thereupon, everyone became very animated, with praise, surprise, and probably relief that they had not said anything derogatory about my drawing while they did not know I spoke their language!

Another time, while I was sketching a bonsai plant in Hangzhou, an elderly workman came up behind me and whispered: "Very good," in perfect English. And then walked away.

Actually, drawing in public is a good opportunity to make friends and meet people. I remember well the nice conversation I had with a young teenager who was out walking the family poodle when he came upon me sketching in the shade of the cathedral of Toledo, Spain. He was very interested in what I was doing and had many questions. I showed him some of my other sketches and I like to fancy that, perhaps in some small ways, I have nurtured in him a taste for architecture, for drawing or, perhaps, a bit of both.

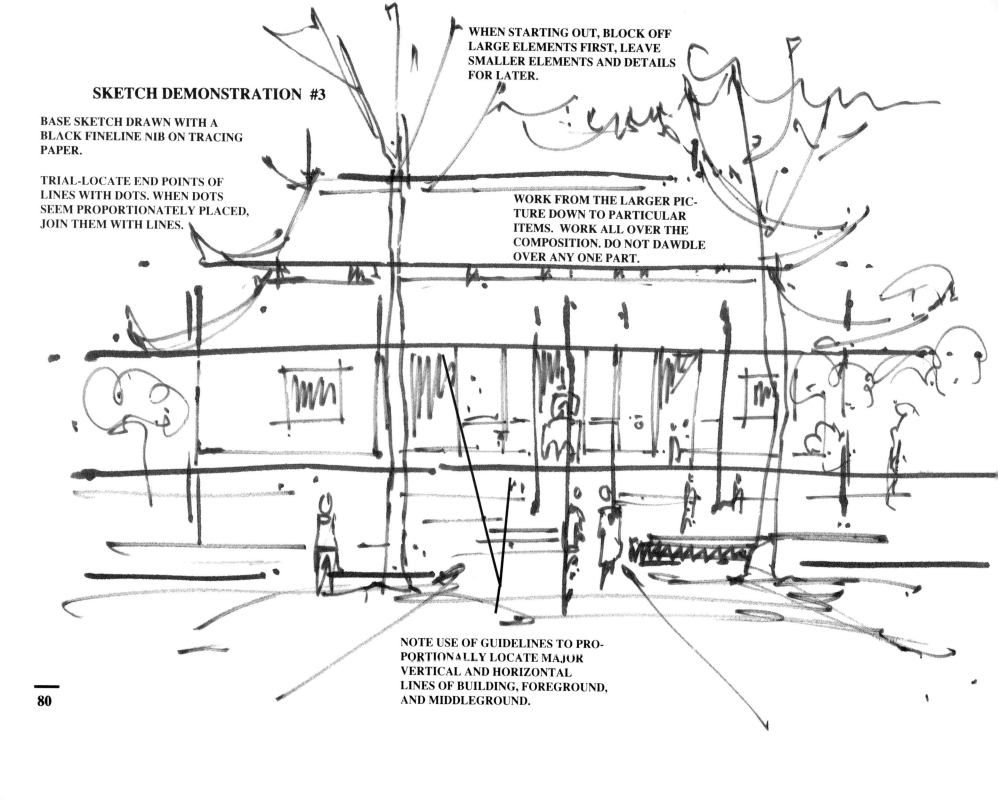

SKETCH DEMONSTRATION #3

WHEN STARTING OUT, BLOCK OFF LARGE ELEMENTS FIRST, LEAVE SMALLER ELEMENTS AND DETAILS FOR LATER.

BASE SKETCH DRAWN WITH A BLACK FINELINE NIB ON TRACING PAPER.

TRIAL-LOCATE END POINTS OF LINES WITH DOTS. WHEN DOTS SEEM PROPORTIONATELY PLACED, JOIN THEM WITH LINES.

WORK FROM THE LARGER PICTURE DOWN TO PARTICULAR ITEMS. WORK ALL OVER THE COMPOSITION. DO NOT DAWDLE OVER ANY ONE PART.

NOTE USE OF GUIDELINES TO PROPORTIONALLY LOCATE MAJOR VERTICAL AND HORIZONTAL LINES OF BUILDING, FOREGROUND, AND MIDDLEGROUND.

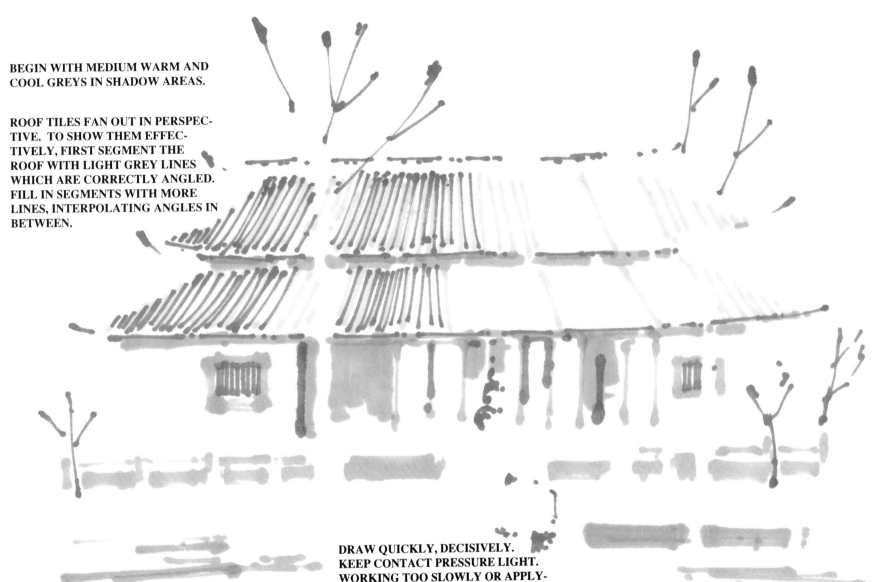

BEGIN WITH MEDIUM WARM AND COOL GREYS IN SHADOW AREAS.

ROOF TILES FAN OUT IN PERSPECTIVE. TO SHOW THEM EFFECTIVELY, FIRST SEGMENT THE ROOF WITH LIGHT GREY LINES WHICH ARE CORRECTLY ANGLED. FILL IN SEGMENTS WITH MORE LINES, INTERPOLATING ANGLES IN BETWEEN.

PAPER IS AQUABEE #638; USED BECAUSE FUZZY MARKER QUALITY ENHANCES CHARACTER OF THIS BUILDING MADE OF ORGANIC MATERIALS.

DRAW QUICKLY, DECISIVELY. KEEP CONTACT PRESSURE LIGHT. WORKING TOO SLOWLY OR APPLYING TOO MUCH PRESSURE WILL CAUSE COLORS TO SPREAD, ESPECIALLY WHEN MARKERS ARE NEW AND FRESH.

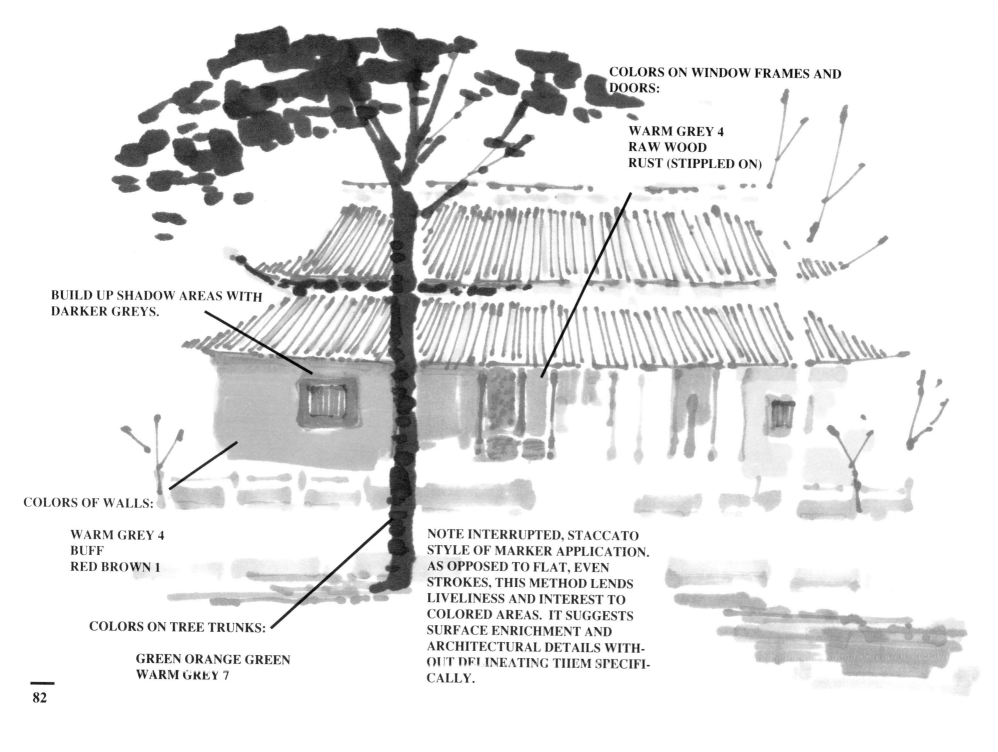

COLORS ON WINDOW FRAMES AND DOORS:

WARM GREY 4
RAW WOOD
RUST (STIPPLED ON)

BUILD UP SHADOW AREAS WITH DARKER GREYS.

COLORS OF WALLS:

WARM GREY 4
BUFF
RED BROWN 1

COLORS ON TREE TRUNKS:

GREEN ORANGE GREEN
WARM GREY 7

NOTE INTERRUPTED, STACCATO STYLE OF MARKER APPLICATION. AS OPPOSED TO FLAT, EVEN STROKES, THIS METHOD LENDS LIVELINESS AND INTEREST TO COLORED AREAS. IT SUGGESTS SURFACE ENRICHMENT AND ARCHITECTURAL DETAILS WITHOUT DELINEATING THEM SPECIFICALLY.

PEOPLE ARE SKETCHED IN WITH
FINE AND ULTRAFINE LINE BLACK,
WITH COLORED CLOTHING FOR
ACCENT. THIS BEING IN CHINA,
CLOTHING COLORS ARE SUBDUED.

COLORS IN FOREGROUND:

WARM GREY 5
GREY 4
GREY 8
GREY 9
GREEN ORANGE GREEN
WILLOW
BEIGE

DEEPEN SHADOWS WITH DARK
GREY AND BLACK.

DRAWING CONVENTIONS

As in the case of most professions or specialized endeavors, designers have developed a unique jargon and some idiosyncracies in expressing themselves and their work. Certain traits permeate drawings that distinctly mark them as having been done by designers, be they architects, landscape architects, or others who are involved with design. Among the traits common to all designers is the propensity to use the line as the primary entity for expression in drawings.

Typically, designers use pen and pencil to draw, which results in drawings in linear form. Lines are used to express the characteristics of objects. With the addition of colors, most visible attributes of a design concept can be represented in a sketch.

The traditional use of lines is being carried on with the advent of felt-tip markers, because markers, like pencils and pens, are linear instruments. They are naturally suited to draw lines.

Sketches by professional designers are evident by the particular ways these people use their drawing instruments. Since markers have characteristics of their own, drawings in this medium by designers can be distinguished by some of the peculiar mannerisms employed.

Maintain a very light contact between marker point and the paper.

Draw rapidly and deliberately.

Tuck little finger under, use it as a glide on the paper, thus controlling distance and contact pressure with the paper.

Keep wrist fairly rigid, bend arm and move hand from the elbow and shoulder.

**HAND AT
START POINT**

**LOOK AT
END POINT**

END POINT

UNINTERRUPTED LINES are drawn
by positioning your marker at the
beginning of a line; look at where you
want your line to end, then let your hand
move to where you are looking. The line
thus drawn would be an uninterrupted
line that appears authoritative and
decisive.

START POINT

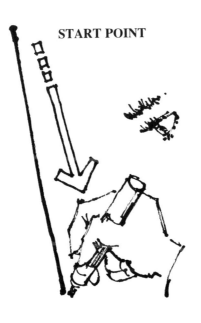

**LET HAND FOLLOW THROUGH
TO WHERE YOU ARE LOOKING**

PRESSURE

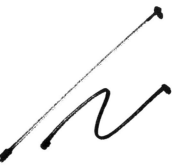

PRESSURE

ACCENTUATED LINES are the very
basic entity used for expressing things in
drawings by designers.

Pressure is applied with a bit of hesitation
at the beginning and end of a line. This
accentuates the line with a little bulb at
the head and tail, making the line more
positive and stronger than a line that just
tapers away.

Different types of lines are used to express different things. Use the type of line that is most in keeping with the nature of the object being drawn.

STRAIGHT LINES are used to draw inorganic objects.

CURVED LINES express organic shapes.

Apply some pressure and deliberateness in drawing **BOLD LINES**. Keep wrist fairly rigid; rotate at elbow and shoulder when drawing long or bold lines.

PARALLEL LINES are used to lend solidity and to enhance the directional character of the object. For example, vertical parallel lines enhance the verticality of a building; curved lines indicate the roundness of rocks, and so forth.

Designers draw with **SPEED** and a certain **NERVOUSNESS** which is reflected in the staccato nature of the lines they draw.

Use light and flickering movement of the fingers when drawing short, **DELICATE LINES.**

CROSS HATCHING with parallel lines is the designer's favorite way to shade a surface, to increase depth or to put more emphasis on a portion of a drawing. The orientation of the crisscross pattern should reflect the character of the surface being expressed.

CENTERLINES and other **GUIDE-LINES** are used to construct drawings. These lines are not erased, so that the visible construction lines are another characteristic of designer drawings.

NOTE: No rulers or other mechanical aids are used in the drawings in this book. Similar to the rationale for limiting the variety of papers and types of markers, I believe it is better to concentrate on the basics and master them before being distracted by too many diversions.

A line is the basic ingredient for sketching used by designers. Lines are used to define shapes and forms, show shades and shadows, textures and surface patterns. Here are some examples.

TEXTURES, PATTERNS

These lines represent the corrugated plastic sheeting of this sign. They are spaced evenly, indicating a man-made object, as differed from a natural, organic surface, which would be more loosely organized.

SPACE AND DISTANCE

Contrasts in value, scale, and relative positions of objects bring out the middle-ground and background.

FORMS AND SHAPES

Lines applied variously delineate the forms and shapes of the subjects.

SHADES AND SHADOWS

Closely spaced lines give the impression of darker shades and deeper shadows than more openly spaced lines.

SHADES AND SHADOWS

Know where light sources are. Light causes shadows, it also affects the intensity of colors. Notice that as surfaces change planes or directions, they appear different in shading and shadowing.

Shadow and surface decor abstractly suggested, not fully delineated.

Note direction of light.

94

SOLIDITY

Solidity can be shown by shading and
shadowing to highlight three-dimensional
qualities. But outlines alone can also
indicate solidity, if they are drawn in
correct proportions and perspective.

All parts have to be seen in context with
the whole picture.

Leaves (intrinsically light) appear heavy
due to massing and dark values.

Stone (intrinsically heavy) seems light
when not in shadow or darkness.

SCALE

Scale is differentiated by the relative weights of lines and elements formed by lines. It is recognized by the juxtaposition of objects in the drawing and the interplay of foreground and background.

Thus a line can be thin as a fishing pole or heavy as a mountain, depending on relative scale and context.

Even if elements are similarly drawn,
relative positions provide clues to the
scale of the objects.

Short, little lines can be windows, ware-
house doors, name of a ship, or homes on
a hillside. It depends on relative positions
and the perception of the viewer.

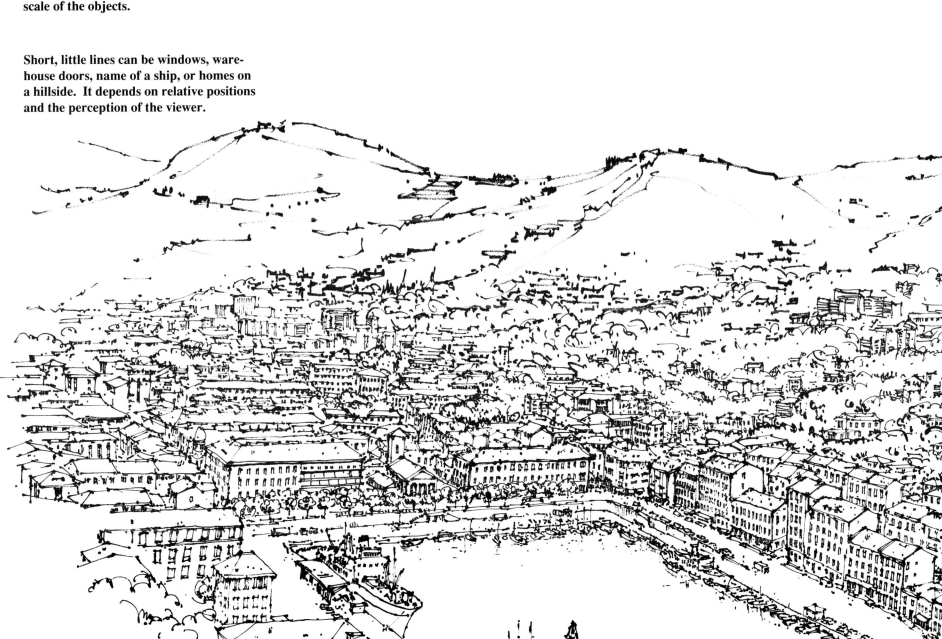

TEXTURES

Draw textures in scale and in keeping
with the character of the real textures.
Even though a texture may be all over an
object, notice how some areas are
bleached out by light or deep in shadow
where the texture is not distinctly visible.

Natural textures are not uniformly
distributed.

Mottled texture is intrinsic in stone.

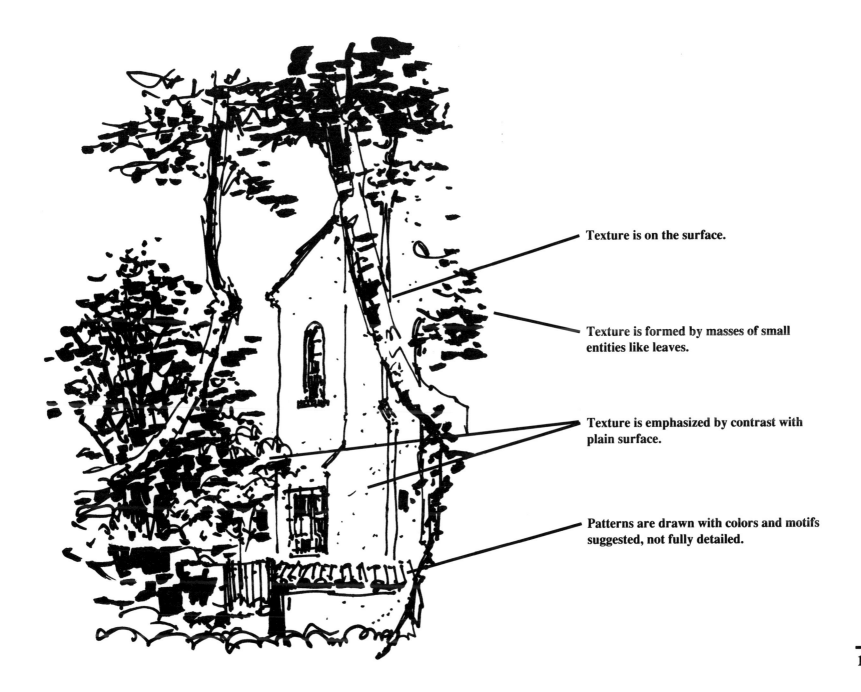

Texture is on the surface.

Texture is formed by masses of small entities like leaves.

Texture is emphasized by contrast with plain surface.

Patterns are drawn with colors and motifs suggested, not fully detailed.

SURFACE ENRICHMENTS

Surface enrichments are most often three-dimensional textures. Draw them to scale and in keeping with the nature of the real object. Draw the shadows cast to bring out the forms and highlights.

Surface patterns from natural materials
and from the way materials are used.

Enrichment applied to surface.

Pattern as a result of construction.

COLORS

Colors, like shades and shadows, change as the angle of view changes. Do not draw in "local" colors. For example, a red chair would not look like it has the same red color throughout. Its color is less intense where light hits most strongly. It has a much darker red in shadow areas and in places where light is blocked. Color values and intensities also change from front to back and from top to bottom.

The ability to differentiate colors, values, textures, and changes in perspective allows us to see real objects and conceptualize ideas in our imagination.

All-white object delineated by:

framing with value contrast

reflected colors

shadows

Contrast between shadows and highlights varies.

Depth of shadows varies.

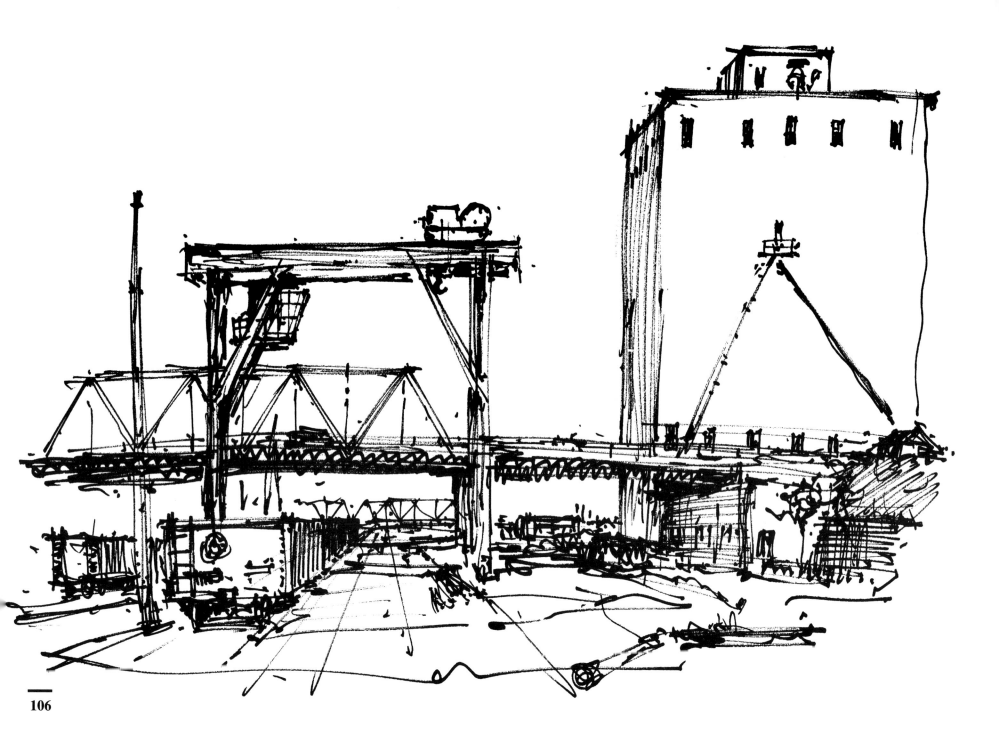

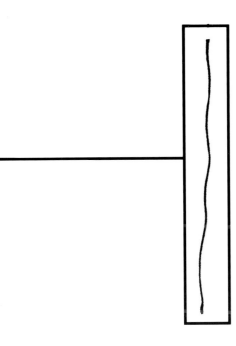

A pictorial element is viewed and drawn in the context of the entire drawing.

Here is a rather organic looking, wavy line. Yet it represents the straight side of a tall building when it is viewed within the framework of the entire sketch.

In this example of a storage building in a rail yard, the sketch was not begun by the drawing of a wavy line or the side of the building. It started with the observation that the building walls were straight, unadorned, and had plain edges. These are the characteristics of the sides of this structure, and a simple line representation of it was drawn. Whether what was drawn is straight enough or properly vertical can only be gauged in the context of the entire drawing.

In this case, the line is more or less vertical, not very straight and generally unadorned. Of course, in an absolute sense, it does not resemble the edge of this building. It is almost impossible to draw absolutely straight lines freehand, anyway. And, I might add, absolutely unnecessary to try. For, in the context of this sketch, where all other elements are not absolutely, mechanically correct, this line is straight enough and plain enough. It is in context, in scale, and in the right position and, therefore, correct and proper.

Drawing in context is particularly relevant to designers because a design is begun by first considering the attributes, parameters, and the characteristics of the object to be designed. Where and how a proposed design is to be used, and by whom is it used are factors that affect the solution to a design problem. The materials to be used, the manner of manufacture, and other attributes of the total context are what a designer has to consider. Sketching is a means of studying the relationships among various aspects of a design and its place in the physical environment.

The content of a designer's sketch is recognizable by the way various attributes of the real objects are drawn.

When a drawing is said to look like the image of a certain object, it is because the object is drawn in the right scale and proportions, shows realistic value contrast and has indications of surface textures. If the object is three dimensional, there should be indications of shades and shadows and some cognizance of solidity. These are the contextual attributes of the object being drawn. If one recognizes an object by its contextual attributes, then it makes sense to begin a drawing by drawing these characteristics. When the attributes are put in context in reference to scale and relative positions, what should emerge is a realistic view of the object being drawn.

To begin a drawing, do not set out to draw any specific object or scene. Start by examining the characteristics of what you see, then try to draw those attributes.

Here are some wriggly lines that are seemingly meaningless. When they are put in context, they become representations of some aspects of the scene being drawn.

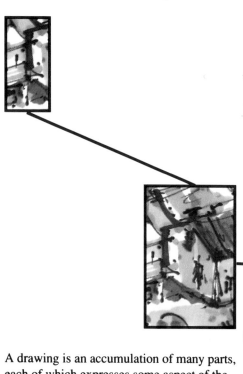

A drawing is an accumulation of many parts, each of which expresses some aspect of the whole and is dependent on the whole to have meaning. This is why you should not do a drawing by completing first one detail, then another. You should work from the larger context to the smaller details. You should work all over the picture field, rather than fixate on any one area.

PORTFOLIO OF SKETCHES

An old maxim asserts that if you want to do something well, you must, first of all, love the subject matter. There must be an empathy towards the architectural surrounding, if you claim to be a designer who deals with that environment. If you like the environment, you will find it infinitely fascinating and full of interesting aspects to contemplate and to elicit through sketches.

There are social aspects, historical references, psychological, and cultural implications. On an aesthetic plane, there are the qualities of light, colors, and the effects of speed on the surrounding. There is the mystery of shades and shadows, and other intangible qualities to draw. There are compositional features such as positive/ negative spatial interaction and perspective angles to consider.

These are facets that can trigger some creative thought. You need only to be open and sensitive to what surrounds you. You need to feel your subject.

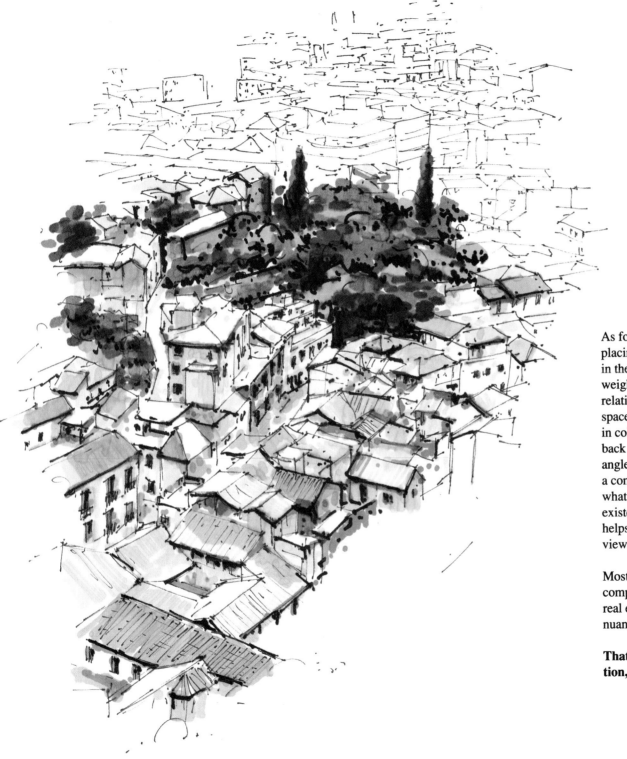

As for composing a sketch, concentrate on placing the elements that are to be included in the picture. Consider balancing the visual weights of the elements. Create a dynamic relationship between positive and negative spaces. Strive for harmony and interaction in colors and values. Consider the front to back movement created by the perspective angle. Keep in mind that what is left out of a composition is sometimes as important as what is put into a picture. The implied existence of something not physically there helps to give a sketch meaning and fires a viewer's imagination.

Most important, in selecting subjects and composing a sketch, you have to observe the real environment and be sensitive to cultural nuances and inter-object relationships.

That you sharpen your sense of observation, is the real value of sketching.

Speed and dexterity in drawing come with practice with familiar equipment and materials.

There is a large variety of marker types: different nibs shapes and sizes, for example, and there is a large variety of papers and surfaces on which to draw. There are also many aids: rulers, marker guides, and masking devices, that artists find useful. Practically speaking, it is well nigh impossible to savor all available materials. Most people rely on a limited range of markers and a few drawing aids that have become familiar to them.

As mentioned, proficiency comes with familiarity. Rather than be distracted by a large variety of markers, papers, or devices, I believe it is better to limit your choices. This way, you will have a chance to become totally at ease with your resources, which will not be possible if you are constantly confronted with new and unfamiliar equipment. Stay with a basic set of materials. Learn to handle them thoroughly before experimenting with something else.

I believe in the basics: practice drawing basic straight lines freehand, and do not rely on a ruler as a crutch; learn to build various shades of colors, rather than buying ready mixed tints.

Rather than literally depicting, object by object, what is in front of you, be selective and include only those aspects that truly express the scene you see.

Recognize the attributes that make up an object. Is the object composed of long or short lines? Does it cut across the picture field? Does it stay in the background or move back and forth? Build up a sketch by expressing these attributes.

At all times, be aware of the total sketch. Think about picture dynamics: balance, movement, and interaction among objects of the picture. Make expressive use of the elements: lines, textures, color and light, solidity, shades and shadows.

Drawing is a way of thinking and a way of looking. It is a mental process as much as it is a manual activity. The trick is not to let the manual or mechanical procedures overshadow the mental process.

Feel what you see and draw what you feel.

Beyond what is physically in the environment — the mountains, trees, buildings, and so forth — there are intangible qualities that give an environment a sense of place. A good sketch elicits this sense rather than simply depicting a collection of objects.

If you are perceptive enough to grasp the fundamental qualities that make up that sense of place, then it is more likely that a viewer will also feel the essence of what you have drawn.

Both the drawing and the viewing of a sketch are matters of perception.

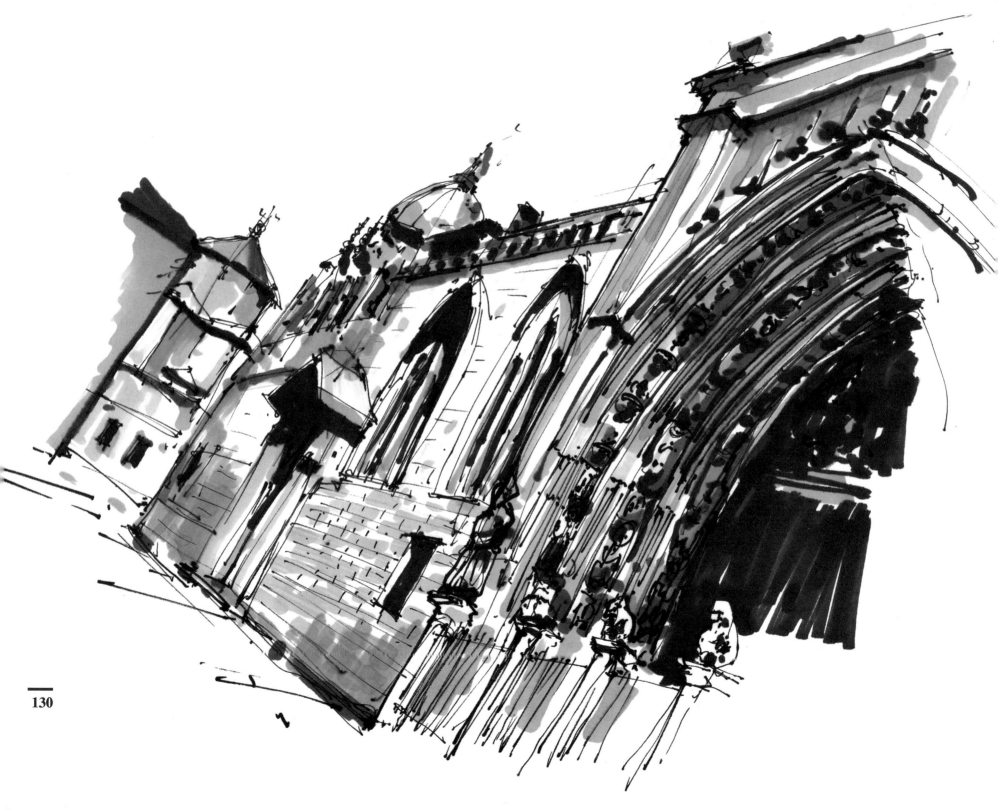

I hope that you will become a better artist by seeing how I draw. In time, you will establish your own style and expressive manners. More important, I have tried to show why I draw. Knowing my reasons for drawing may lead you to become more aware of the architectural environment.

What is built is indicative of the values of human society. City planning, building siting, and the way interior spaces are organized, are all reflections of how a society functions. They should be valid objects of concern for you who are in a position to affect that environment, whether as a professional designer, an artist, or as a concerned citizen.

Your awareness can surely help to make this world a better place for everyone.

LIST OF ILLUSTRATIONS

Page	Title and Location	Original Image Size	% Printed

PORTFOLIO OF SKETCHES

Page	Title and Location	Original Image Size	% Printed
110 - 111	Three Churches, Logroño	18" x 8"	80%
112	Cathedral Facade, Santiago de Compostela, Spain	9" x 12"	64%
113	View from the Alhambra, Granada	10" x 11"	70%
114	Hillside, Estella, Spain	9.5" x 6"	74%
115	Houses, Estella	10.5" x 7"	100%
116	Interior, Versailles, France	6.5" x 5"	100%
117	Barrio Santa Cruz, Córdoba	7.5" x 10"	75%
118	Li River, Guilin	11" x 8"	90%
119	Happy Valley, Hong Kong	12" x 9"	80%
120	Fishing Village, Shenzhen	11" x 9"	90%
121	Village, near Barcelona, Spain	19" x 10"	58½%
122	Bonsai 3, Hangzhou	9" x 7"	100%
123	Bonsai 4, Hangzhou	9" x 7"	100%
124	Cathedral Spire, Sevilla	7" x 10"	75%
125	Torre Molinos, Malága, Spain	7" x 7.5"	94%
126	Behind Cathedral, Pamplona	11" x 8"	90%
127	House, Santo Tomas de Ollas, Spain	9.5" x 7"	100%
128	Old Church, Segovia, Spain	8" x 5.5"	100%
129	City Square, Lugo, Spain	10.5" x 7.5"	100%
130	Cathedral Side, Toledo	7" x 10"	75%
131	Houses, Ronda	7" x 7.5"	65%
132	Cathedral, Burgos	13" x 9"	41%
133	Over View, Segovia	18" x 11"	60%
134	Ile Saint Louis, Paris, France	9" x 9"	90%
135	Convento de San Benito, Estella	10.5" x 8"	100%
136	Santa Susana, Santiago de Compostela	8" x 10"	65%
137	Castillo, Ponferrada, Spain	9" x 6"	100%
138 - 139	Cathedral, Santiago de Compostela	13" x 7"	100%

BIBLIOGRAPHY

Abercrombie, S. 1984. *Architecture as Art*, New York: Van Nostrand Reinhold.

Atkin, William W. 1976. *Architectural Presentation Techniques*, New York: Van Nostrand Reinhold.

Attoe, Wayne. 1978. *Architecture and Critical Imagination*, New York: John Wiley & Sons.

Brolin, Brent C. 1980. *Architecture in Context,* New York: Van Nostrand Reinhold.

Ching, Francis D.K. 1979. *Architecture: Form, Space & Order*, New York: Van Nostrand Reinhold.

Ching, Francis D.K. 1990. *Drawing, A Creative Approach*, New York: Van Nostrand Reinhold.

Colletti, Jack J. and Paul J., eds. 1974. *Freehand Approach to Technical Drawing*, Englewood Cliffs, NJ: Prentice-Hall.

Crowe, Norman and Lasean, Paul. 1984. *Visual Notes for Architects and Designers,* New York: Van Nostrand Reinhold.

Deasy, C.M. 1974. *Design for Human Affairs*, New York: John Wiley & Sons.

Deasy, C.M. and Lasswell, T.E. 1985. *Designing Places for People*, New York: John Wiley & Sons.

Doyle, Michael. 1979. *Color Drawing*, New York: Van Nostrand Reinhold.

Drpic, Ivo D. 1988. *Sketching and Rendering Interior Spaces*, New York: Whitney Library of Design.

Ellis, Russell and Cuff, Dana, eds. 1989. *Architects' People*, New York: Oxford University Press.

Evans, Ray. 1983. *Drawing and Painting Architecture*, New York: Van Nostrand Reinhold.

Giedion, Sigfried. 1971. *Architecture and the Phenomena of Transition*, Cambridge, MA: Harvard University Press.

Halse, Albert O. 1988. *Architectural Rendering, 3rd Ed.*, New York: McGraw Hill.

Hatch, C. Richard, ed. 1984. *The Scope of Social Architecture*, New York: Van Nostrand Reinhold.

Hesselgren, Sven. 1975. *Man's Perception of Man-Made Environment*, Stroudsburg, PA: Dowden, Hutchinson & Ross.

Heuser, Karl R. 1980. *Freehand Drawing and Sketching,* New York: Van Nostrand Reinhold.

Hoffpauir, Stephen and Rosner, Joyce. 1989. *Architectural Illustration in Watercolor*, New York: Whitney Library of Design.

Jacoby, Helmut. 1981. *New Techniques of Architecutral Rendering, 2nd Ed.*, New York: Van Nostrand Reinhold.

Joedicke, Jürgen. 1985. *Space and Form in Architecture*, Stuttgart: Karl Kramer Verlag.

Kliment, Stephen, ed. 1984. *Architectural Sketching and Rendering*, New York: Whitney Library of Design.

Kuckein, H.E. 1984. *Architectural Illustration and Presentation*, Reston/Prentice-Hall.

Lam, Christopher M.C. 1977. *Perception and Lighting as Formgivers for Architecture*, New York: McGraw-Hill.

Lang, Jon. 1987. *Creating Architectural Theory*, New York: Van Nostrand Reinhold.

Leach, Sid D.M. 1978. *Techniques of Interior Design and Presentation*, New York: McGraw-Hill.

Lockard, William Kirby. 1974. *Design Drawing/Design Drawing Experiences*, Tucson, AZ: Pepper Publishing Company.

Mikellides, B., ed. 1980. *Architecture for People*, New York: Holt, Rinehart and Winston.

Mori, Takashi. 1982. *Perspective Rendering for Commercial Design (Interiors)*, New York: Van Nostrand Reinhold.

Oliver, Robert S. 1989. *The Complete Sketch*, New York: Van Nostrand Reinhold.

Oliver, Robert S. 1979. *The Sketch*, New York: Van Nostrand Reinhold.

Oliver, Robert S. 1983. *The Sketch in Color*, New York: Van Nostrand Reinhold.

Passini, Romedi. 1984. *Wayfinding in Architecture*, New York: Van Nostrand Reinhold.

Prak, Niels L. 1984. *Architects: the Noted and the Ignored*, New York: John Wiley & Sons.

Rapoport, Amos. 1982. *The Meaning of the Built Environment*, Beverly Hills, CA: Sage.

Scruton, Roger. 1979. *The Aesthetics of Architecture*, Princeton, NJ: Princeton University Press.

Severino, Renato. 1970. *Equipotential Space*, New York: Praeger.

Smithies, K.W. 1981. *Principles of Design in Architecture*, New York:

Sommer, Robert. 1972. *Design Awareness*, Corte Madera, CA: Rinehart Press.

Sommer, Robert. 1983. *Social Design: Creating Buildings with People in Mind*, Englewood Cliffs, NJ: Prentice-Hall.

Thiis-Evensen, Thomas. 1989. *Archetypes in Architecture*, New York: Oxford University Press.

Van der Ven, Cornelis. 1977. *Space in Architecture*, Assen, The Netherlands: Van Gorcum & Company.

Venturi, Robert and Brown, Denise Scott. 1984. *A View from the Campidoglio*, New York: Harper & Row.

Wang, Thomas C. 1977. *Pencil Sketching*, New York: Van Nostrand Reinhold.

Wang, Thomas C. 1981. *Sketching with Markers*, New York: Van Nostrand Reinhold.

Wells, Melcolm. 1981. *Gentle Architecture*, New York: McGraw-Hill.

Willis, Lucy. 1988. *Light: How to See It, How to Paint It*, Cincinnati, OH: North Light Books.

Williams, A. Richard. 1980. *A Reflexion of Architecture and Urban Design*, San Francisco, CA: Center for Architecture and Urban Studies, distributors.

INDEX